DON'T YOU CRY
I'M ON VENUS

SAID NOTHING. MEDIA

DON'T YOU CRY I'M ON VENUS

LAYLA SAID NOTHING

Copyright © 2025 Layla Elena Said
All rights reserved.

ISBN 979-8-218-37116-6

Library of Congress Control Number: 2024905772

Written by Layla Said Nothing
@laylasaidnothing

Published in the United States by
Said Nothing. Media LLC

A home for poetry in all its forms.

www.saidnothing.media

a present to my younger self

CONTENTS

ENTER: WAR ZONE

ROCKY MOUNTAIN LAKE 2

A. NERVOSA 3

SUNGOD 4

DAILY NEWS 5

BOYS WILL BE BOYS 6

DIRTY 8

WEEK IN REVIEW 10

MAMIKA 12

BLUEBIRD 14

SMALLTALK 16

ODE TO SUN 17

LEAVE: WAR ZONE

FREEDOM DOESN'T MEAN FREE 20

CHARLOTTE'S WEB 21

RESISTANCE 22

MOTHER 23

HERSTORY 24

MAGDALENE 26

MISCARRIAGE 27

YOU TELL ME 28

EPISODE IV 30

OLD HABITS 32

CHRISTINA'S WORLD 33

GROUP THERAPY 34

LITHIUM 35

SINGULARITY 36

DEW AT DAWN 38

ENTER: MYSELF

DON'T YOU CRY, I'M ON VENUS 42

THE COLOR YELLOW 46

BAD POEM 48

PULP DICTION 49

RELIEF 50

LIFE'S A BITCH 52

REASON 54

SHE WHO LAUGHS LAST 56

IDENTITY 57

UNSEX ME HERE 58

ALREADY DEAD 60

NOTES 63

ACKNOWLEDGMENTS 65

ABOUT THE AUTHOR 66

DON'T YOU CRY

I'M ON VENUS

LAYLA SAID NOTHING

ENTER: WAR ZONE

ROCKY MOUNTAIN LAKE

I love to watch geese flapping above until
I worry they'll shit on my head.
Kids play innocently outside

inside of a past where
they aren't shot dead.
All of them are white.

A woman jogs with anxiety and pepper spray
to care for the body her husband ignores.
The older, wiser woman knows to ride a bike.

A girl smokes her pipe on a bench
dreaming into the Rockies
she knows will be bullied to dust.

She waits to leave until
the jogger returns to safety.

A. NERVOSA

A pot-bellied parasite cuts
Louder than the bones in my wrist jut

She's gutted a hole
She seeks control

Tighter than stark ribs lie
Through gritted teeth

Against this thinly curtained flesh.
I need to purge her faster than she feeds

On the weight of my stomach but
Then I'd have to take a bite and

I'm just not that hungry.

SUNGOD

The only way I can close my eyes
and still know where I'm going
is if I'm looking for the sun.

They blink to bow
while painting the fresh
orange color of blood.

If I were to open my eyes –
I'd blind.
I'm still repenting the last time I tried.

No one has permission inside
the goldenrod iris of god.

DAILY NEWS

We have numbed ourselves to survive yet
our insensitivity is killing us.

Family home videos?
Those aren't even real anymore.

Fake News:
This Year More Children Were Shot In School
Than Graduated From It

Real News:
Man Shoots Family Because
He Loves Them

Remember the two atomic bombs?
Is that why Americans love fighting cancer?

Oh, and
the doctor called back -

You aren't sick,
just dying.

empty.
a golden goose gutted for eggs:
> *was your cotton-mouthed animal*
> *quenched when I bled?*

reluctantly she spreads her legs to feel
his fullness, yet she only feels
emptiness.

BOYS WILL BE BOYS

DIRTY

I am sitting in a bath soaking in my filth. That should tell you something. The page should be dry except I let it get wet, even though the tree already washed it with her tears.

My words are bleeding through the page, I fear they will never be read.

I should just throw the book away. I shouldn't have even brought it here in the first place, but I can't. I have to tell you something.

My succulent died and I
blamed it on the nameless sun, though
she was never meant to survive.

I treat a yellow like a green
I haven't shaved my vagina in eight weeks
I curse too much and swear too little
I have cavities from all the coke
I overdosed and made a joke, *too soon!*
I have terrible timing.

A ship in a bottle
I waterboard my papered tongue
yet it is always dry
I don't know why
I am manic.

I have to tell you something.

I want to sink
down in this water
the way you drown into a dream,
or so I am told, except

I'm dirty
and
the water isn't clean.

WEEK IN REVIEW

Mondays you look in the mirror and scream at the wrinkle on your forehead. Age is your enemy.

Tuesdays you obsess over why he hasn't texted you back yet, even though you swear you've played it all perfectly.

Wednesdays you cry incessantly because your mother stopped calling and you're scared that she won't have it all before she dies. Mostly you're not really sure why you're crying.

Thursdays you feel fat even though the scale reads 116. Maybe that's why he hasn't called you back?

Fridays you play dress up so you can feel like the most beautiful woman in the world for men who couldn't care less.

Saturdays you work anxiously on side projects you pray will give your life purpose, except you can never quite seem to finish.

Sundays you pace. You don't go to church because there isn't one for you, but you pray anyway, deeply. You ask god for forgiveness because, despite all that She has given you, you can't find one day to be grateful.

MAMIKA

I never got to mourn my grandmother because
I'm not even sure if she's dead, except
I'm sure she is.

Mother doesn't like to talk about it.
I know that because when I ask,
she shuts me up
she shuts herself down
she shuts Mamika out.

I reach inside to find the words to say goodbye
but I'm as empty as the cookie jar.

We parted ways on a day
we didn't know would be our last.
My mind skips rocks across the surface of our past
like that time before I left summer camp.
I never went back.

Last time I left to see her in Brooklyn,
I never made it into the building.
It wasn't safe enough to leave the car.

My last memory of her
was in that fifth-floor window,

a shadow dancing behind the curtains
singing in Romanian
cooking us cabbage soup.

BLUEBIRD

I

The girl nervously twirls her curls
so they will be bouncy enough
for him. The devil cursed her
with mother's frizz,
She could never quite overcome
the madness.

She asked herself questions like:

>   *If 'is' is a verb,*
>
>   *Why do 'his' words not move?*

She prayed to know how it felt

>   to be
>
>   *the only girl in his room.*

II

The other day she heard her mother crying
the potent hues of Guernica
splattered against the backdrop
of a drowning bluebird.

In between her mother's hollow gasps

    she heard her ask:

        Why do 'his' words not move?

She prayed to know how it felt

    to be

        free, in her own room.

SMALLTALK

Let's talk about the weather today –

I heard Thunder
is a woman with braided hair
screaming from the bottom of a well,
her hungry cells clicking like cottonmouth
killing to powder her nose in blue ecstasy –
This is how she awakens the sky.

Let's talk about the weather today –

Life pushed me in the pool so I could learn
how to swim and I drowned. Down down
gurgling Thunder's powdered crown
folding like milkweed into autumn.

And while I helplessly bled out of air
the earth dried out of her water.

ODE TO SUN

Her beams melt kindly,
Like orange creamsicle
Into nectarine daydreams

She showers sins with virgin sweat
Like holy water. Reborn a sun:
I am her daughter.

Molting memories from skin
She toasts his ultraviolence
With ultraviolets.

Her burns cauterized the sense of self
Hemorrhaging since my homicide because
I died that night

Then her citrusy clockwork
Kissed me like sunrise
Fusing me softly to life.

LEAVE: WAR ZONE

FREEDOM DOESN'T MEAN FREE

It's Independence Day and
we're quarantined in the homes
we can no longer afford.

I feel free enough to burn the flag.
Police drag us by the hair
as we protest their violence at The Capitol.

George Washington stands marbled
covered in blood, debating the spectacle
like an Oxford comma.

I find myself asking:

Is this anarchy
or democracy?

What kind of freedom
doesn't mean free?

What kind of freedom means
we can't breathe?

CHARLOTTE'S WEB

What webs we write
Within the words we weave when

Goodbye really meant I would stay
And stay always meant you would leave.
Naïve only begins to explain –

I want to write like Charlotte

Wash myself clean of your sticky fingers
Bleach the scent of you that lingers
Worse than an awkward silence

Unravel kindness from
your subtle emotional violence.

I want to write like Charlotte

Let these words survive
As proof, even though
Her silver-dusted rain dance
Told far more truth.

RESISTANCE

I choked on your eyelash from that butterfly kiss.
I wish I never missed the foreshadowing.

A nesting doll
you broke my will

one by one until
the personal became political.

The way you claimed me in your solar system
then disregarded me like Pluto

when you never even felt like home,
when I never even asked to be a planet.

MOTHER

Sidewalk cracks
I skipped for you
as if latently
I feared yet knew
our time would soon be done

So as I walked
I watched my feet,
taking wide steps
or two as one.

Where did you wander, or
did you run? Door locked
before tossing the key.

Now older I walk
watching my feet
as I search the cracks
tirelessly.

HERSTORY

He shakes me like a broken doll
when I don't perform to function
as though
hitting the computer
ever really got it started.

He tells me I talk too much
about feelings
as though
sex does not require intimacy.

He tells me he's too busy
as though
I'm studying the economic uncertainty of
waiting for him to kiss me

as though
I'm conducting a marginal analysis of
self-worth per unit of affection

as though
my book writes itself while I sleep

as though
my thoughts are the ocean
just only dick deep.

He tells me to
write him a poem
as though

I got back up
and fell
and got back up
and fell
and got back up

to write *his* story
instead of *my* history,

the kind that wildfires tell.

I've watched you cower long
Behind slick teeth

That chewed my seven devils
As you grinned

How fruitless since
You damned me with those lips

(If a man I'd be absolved of sin)

A withered flax
Just waiting to be skinned

A flower floundered with
Her back against the wind

He will be the death of me

MAGDALENE

MISCARRIAGE

My daughter's blood
still stains his sheets,
wrinkled like the one
that lined my mother's womb.

He hasn't even bothered to wash them.
He hasn't even asked how I'm doing.

Instead, he whimpers like an injured dog
to an unforgiving moon, half-baked
tangled in another woman's flesh

pretending it was all just a
period

and not the death of a
lifetime

YOU TELL ME

Everyone feels it
Yet nobody knows what it is

It is trapped in a bottle
pressurized to explode
Its message encrypted in binary code
I'm starting to think
in ones_and_zeros.

It is a game
with players unnamed
You don't know you're playing
until you are played.
It doesn't play fair.

It is a penny
for the old guy
at the expense of his child
who now vapes Black & Milds for breakfast.

It is the ring-around-the-rosie
     the ring around the turtle's neck
     the ring from an unknown caller

Don't answer!
It'll kill you.

EPISODE IV

Madness
is burying yourself
inside your head
a good idea?

I forgot
        The world isn't real
              I can't feel it anymore

             When I punch myself in the head

    I do not yell
                  I scream

        In my lucid dreams

                      I beg

     The doctors

                        Kill me,

please.

OLD HABITS

Sometimes you have to
exorcise the sadness
and relieve yourself of madness.

That's why I keep
scissors in my nightstand.

CHRISINA'S WORLD

Left alone to parch among the grass
Taunted by the static of the blades
Their hissing cuts like snakes of broken glass
Christina, would you like to die today?

Her hellish pasture chains without escape
Betrayed by legs that gave out long ago
Strangled by this monochrome it rapes
The color from the very world she knows

The young cicadas chirp her elegy
Its timbre bleeds a melancholic gray
The same shade as her earthly canopy
She hums along the song they sing to say -

Christina, you would like to die today.
Christina, you would like to die today.

GROUP THERAPY

Action combined with distraction
Bodies void of satisfaction
Horror stories, faded glories

What pushed us to the brink?

Confusion merging with delusion
Staring blankly at this page
Medicated and sedated, I think –

All the ward's a stage.

LITHIUM

Head cloudy.
Thoughts once loud
are humming proudly.

I'm learning
it takes pain to heal pain

I'm yearning
for control of my own brain

I'm tired
of feeling insane
of side effects
outweighing the gains.

...

If my mind were a season
it'd be a cool summer rain.

SINGULARITY

I don't know how to write anymore.
I stopped thinking in verse
I stopped breathing in song
Where has she gone, and why for so long?

A black hole:
Where light and sound cannot escape
Where particles evaporate
With Hawking radiation.

      I wonder how Steph came to this theory
      If he was thinking about love
      even subconsciously
      As he blinded himself
      Staring into her event horizon
      Even though they always told him:
      Never look directly into the sun.

      But without sight, it was too late
      She swallowed his light

She hollowed his shape
Collapsing his weight into singularity -
A pupil of infinite density
In the eye of her beautiful storm.

And that was his epiphany:
Stop looking when you find
The one who pauses space and time.
And even though it can't last forever,
At least you'll evaporate
happily together.

I found my singularity.
I found my voice again.
Pressed like an ocean
In the blue of my pen.

DEW AT DAWN

There is a reason grass has no thorns:
It welcomes.

Blades flickered in the wind and smiled, as though the earth were reflecting the stars. The ground, a cool rippling pool of seafoam.

I dive in headfirst. Not pausing to see my reflection; not stopping to take off my clothes. There is no time for subtleties.

I chew my way through roots, through dirt. Washing them down with groundwater. Digging deeper and deeper within myself, searching for the inflection where

dawn melts kindly into dusk and
stars make magic out of dust.

ENTER: MYSELF

DON'T YOU CRY, I'M ON VENUS

ENTER: WAR ZONE

>A class divided in opposing battle
>I sit alone on the front line.
>Mind you, I didn't volunteer -
>I was drafted.
>A moon-faced baby
>I can't shave my legs let alone
>hold a gun.
>Bullied to a pulp,
>teacher sends me home to practice algebra.

LEAVE: WAR ZONE

>But you never really leave a war zone.
>Laughs echo like a firing squad
>to curse me an insomniac.
>A moon-faced girl
>I press my face against the mirror and stare,
>not more than three inches between us:
>the girl I see and the one inside me.
>I stay glued here for years while
>we separate like mitosis

Not pretty enough for a girl
I must be a boy or a dog, but
I walk on two legs
and I don't want to play dead,
I want to shower in acid
 and dissolve my head.

ENTER: MYSELF

The blue lady sits in lotus
giving the OK;
the sun crowns her head
like the Madonna.

The past lingers
like the dirty secret of a fallen angel
who keeps postponing her funeral,
but now, like the sunflower,
I surrender to the sun. Now,
nowhere in my lexicon is sorry because
wildfires don't breathe the language of apology.

So don't you cry for me,
I'm on Venus.

THE COLOR YELLOW

My first baby's breath was yellow, back when I was happiest and wanted to be a horticulturist - I was four.

My mother Brindusa (brin-doo-sha) was my first best friend. A tired woman, who waitressed across the street. At the *click* of the door, I'd run to stand on the couch to reach the little window and watch her wave across the universe. I'd whisper to the honeybees who shared our window until she returned. Their amber hive dripped of liquid promise.

I wake up on a planet with no color and ask if I've become the Little Prince. No, but I must find him somewhere. Except I recollect his golden hair, and I'm lost in a field of wheat. And I can't bear to see the snake, so I drift helplessly asleep.

Back on earth, it's worse. I hide under covers to escape daylight. Under the space for favorite color, I write: none. I find it pointless that we should prefer one. My mother and I don't talk, we *Yell*. I know inside that I am sick, so she takes my temperature: 98.6. But I feel it rotting in my head, so we *Yell* until we paint it red.

The canary is me but I'm trapped in his mine. I try to scream *danger,* but I've run out of time. A cherry paints the canvas red. I learn how girls feel playing dead.

The *Brindusa* is a flower known for its ability to thrive in late winter. She grows in purple, white, and yellow. I was birthed from this flower, like lemons squeeze for lemonade, I am a shade of yellow I made.

BAD POEM

Words that once knitted themselves
into cozy sweaters
have been foaming at the mouth.
The ink from my pen

was a fountain of life, now
I have to think twice
before writing at all.

It's a tall order
to write
A Good Poem.

The more art becomes a chore
the further we have drifted from
our own humanity.

I won't call her dead -
I know she is here, with me,
as long as I'm still breathing.

PULP DICTION

The same day Sylvia Plath became my dictionary
I realized - I didn't need you.

Strip me of bones but
              leave the olive folds of skin

Set fire to them and
              leave the ashes for the wind

Or, I'll rip you with my teeth
Just to see

If the pulp of you tastes ripe as fiction
The kind that bites like Sylvia's diction.

RELIEF

I wanted to die today
planned my funeral and my wake
mapped what everyone would say
topographically.

The mountains my mother
concentric and steep
angular by nature
echoes like orca
crying for young
the avalanche would break her.

Plateau my sister
shrugs her shoulders
curling her raised lips
That selfish girl thought of herself
just as she always did.

The empty plains my younger sis
would hollow in her pain
though whispers rustle leaves of grass
she'd never sing again.

I wanted to die today but
my brother the cascade
would drown the western coast,
he'd flood the continent with tears
(I think of him the most).

He wouldn't understand how death
removes one from the map,
He's the reason the verb *want*
is structured in the past.

LIFE'S A BITCH

Wore a smile as my disguise
Through the madness and dying inside

Left for Venus the stars as my guide
Didn't think I'd make it alive

Met a woman with diamonds for eyes
Crystals fell from her face as she cried

Told me *'honey, stop wasting your time*
Life's a bitch, and then you die -

Take me as I am
Leave the pieces where you can

Didn't have a plan
Packed my bag, 30 minutes and I ran

I don't need a man
Rather catch a starship with an alien

You don't understand
I'd rather be alone than on demand.

People ask what I am
Human, Romanian, and Afghan

Sometimes I felt like an alien
Stuck on Earth, looking for my homeland

Like a ship in the sand
In a bottle, doing all that I can

To be free from the script, come with me
And return to the ocean.

REASON

Find me a more obscure word than "reason"
Find me a feeling that lasts longer than a season
      a wave who crashes in silence
      a body without a scar
      a scar without violence.

Find me two pieces of sand the same shade
      the best laid plan, no mistakes

Find me someone who gives more than they take
      and does so selflessly.

Find me a book read once without a crease
Find me an extra week a month or
      a finder who never seeks.

Find me an ending that never had a start
Find me a love that
      doesn't end with a broken heart.

SHE WHO LAUGHS LAST

Take me to the day we met
So I can run the other way and then
I'll never dare look back again
You painted me in gray and when

I tried to leave, I stayed
Not sure why I played
The games that you made,
Lost in a daze
Not sure why I laid
In the grave that you paved.

I've made my mistakes
I've felt my heart break but
She who laughs last
Laughs best anyway.

IDENTITY

Don't look at me like you know me -
I don't even know me.

Topography finds
relief in each line
the way a tree grows
one leaf at a time.

If I died suddenly,
would you cry for me?

If I could be anything,
I'd choose to be free.

UNSEX ME HERE

I don't really care
about anything

                              I bow in prayer
                            here for everything

My mind is aware
she has diamond wings

                              Life isn't fair
                            guess I'll kill the king

This is my life
if I do it right
won't do it twice

                              Pen for a knife
                            will kill the king
                                before I die

He is not mine

                    I don't follow his rules

        I won't swallow his wine.

Unsex me here

             Take me to paradise.

At Me	You look
The Ghost	Of Man
See Me	You Can't
The Wind	I Am

If I Said

Face Me	You Won't
Know Me	You Don't
I'm Living	As Though
I'm Already	Dead

NOTES

"Mamika" is dedicated to my grandmother, Elena, who shares my middle name and deep love of poetry.

"Bluebird" recalls the painting *Guernica* by Pablo Picasso.

"Charlotte's Web" references E.B. White's book of the same name.

"Christina's World" is an ekphrasis poem inspired by Andrew Wyeth's painting of the same name.

"The Color Yellow" borrows language and themes from 'The Little Prince' in the second stanza, a wonderful book by Antoine de Saint-Exupéry.

"Pulp Diction" references Sylvia Plath, my favorite poet.

"Life's a Bitch" was originally released as a song on the EP *Poetry is Not A Luxury*.

"She Who Laughs Last" was originally released as a music single in 2024.

NOTES

"Unsex Me Here" was originally released as a song on the EP *Poetry is Not A Luxury*. The line is borrowed from the play Macbeth by William Shakespeare.

Music can be accessed on Spotify, Apple Music, SoundCloud, Amazon Music, and other streaming platforms @laylasaidnothing.

ACKNOWLEDGEMENTS

Thank you to my mother, for her love of learning and literature. For showing me that with hard work and a strong moral compass, anything is possible. For each of my siblings, this holds true.

Thank you to my friend, AJ, for taking the time to workshop many of these poems with me. I appreciate your love for the craft and unwavering belief in my art since that first poetry class at Penn State.

Thank you to Shara McCallum, my first poetry professor, and the first person to call me a poet. Your belief in me fueled my belief in myself. Convinced me I was "good enough." That gift to a writer is invaluable. Thank you for creating a space in that classroom and your office hours for me to unravel the concepts which became this book of poems.

Thank you to the friends who have supported my poetry and inspired me along the way.

Thank you to those who took the time to get to know this book, a child of my experience and my creation.

ABOUT THE AUTHOR

Layla Said Nothing is an Afghan Romanian American who started writing poems at the age of six. In 2022, she released two EPs titled *Portrait of a Young Woman* and *Poetry is Not A Luxury*. In 2025 she published her first collection of poems, *Don't You Cry, I'm on Venus*.

Layla has raised over $2.7 million to prevent and end homelessness for youth in her community. Her work has been featured in Tagg Magazine, FOX31, 9News, Axios, The Colorado Sun, CBS, Denverite, and Westword.

Learn more about Layla and her poetry at www.saidnothing.media.

SAID NOTHING. MEDIA

LAYLA SAID NOTHING

GO TO VENUS

www.ingramcontent.com/pod-product-compliance
Lightning Source LLC
Chambersburg PA
CBHW021950160426
43195CB00011B/1305